Young Runemasters Guide To Rune Casting And Rune Magic

WRITTEN & ILLUSTRATED BY

Veronica Fowler

March 2020

In early 2019, after Veronica's young son took an interest in her books about Norse Paganism and Runes, she decided to create a book that was at his reading level.

Veronica has been writing for 20+ years and has natural artistic abilities. Her other interests include singing, fishing and being outdoors.

This book is a sequel to her first book titled:

Children's Book of Runes

Follow & find out more at:

http://www.amazon.com/author/veronicafowler

Table of Contents

Creating Your Set of Runes	4
Casting	6
• Throwing	7
• Rune Spreads	10
Rune Magic	18
• Talismans & Amulets	20
• Runic Formulas	25
Murkstave Runes	26
Rune Reference Pages	27-28
Alphabet Reference	29

Creating Your Set of Runes

(Read this book in its' entirety before attempting Castings and Magic)

Before creating your own set of runes, make sure that you have an adult ready to help you, if needed. Sharp tools and finishes containing chemicals may be required, depending on the material you choose to create your runes with.

When you create your own set of runes, you put a little bit of yourself into them. Some Runemasters even sew their own pouch or bag, or carve a wooden box, to keep their runes in.

Your runes can be made out of stones, molded out of clay or carved out of small wood slices. On stones, you can use red enamel paint to draw each rune onto one stone. Red is the traditional color used for runes. The stones you use can be evenly rounded, polished crystals or river stones that are about one inch in diameter. This will be the easiest technique. If you choose to mold with clay, you can make a smooth circle, oval or square, that is a quarter to a half inch thick and two inches in diameter. Before the clay dries, carve each rune into the clay. Once it's dry, paint inside the rune with red enamel paint. Or you can let it dry, without carving the rune, and paint the rune on the smooth surface of the clay instead. Once the paint is dry, spray it with a clear coat spray paint. If you choose to use wood slices, you will want to find a fallen branch from a hard wood tree that is about one inch in diameter. Slice the wood a quarter to a half inch thick. Wooden runes need to be sanded smooth before being carved into or painted on. You may choose to carve your rune into each slice, then paint inside the rune, or simply paint on the smooth surface. Once the paint dries, stain each piece with your choice of wood stain on both sides for a finished look. You may be able to find pre-cut wood slices at your local craft store.

Once your set is finished, meditate with each rune, separately, putting your energy into them. In your mind, picture the rune that you are holding and recite the meanings to yourself. You can ask Odin to bless your runes and guide you when you use them. This will help you memorize each rune and bond them to you. Do not let anyone else touch or use your runes after this.

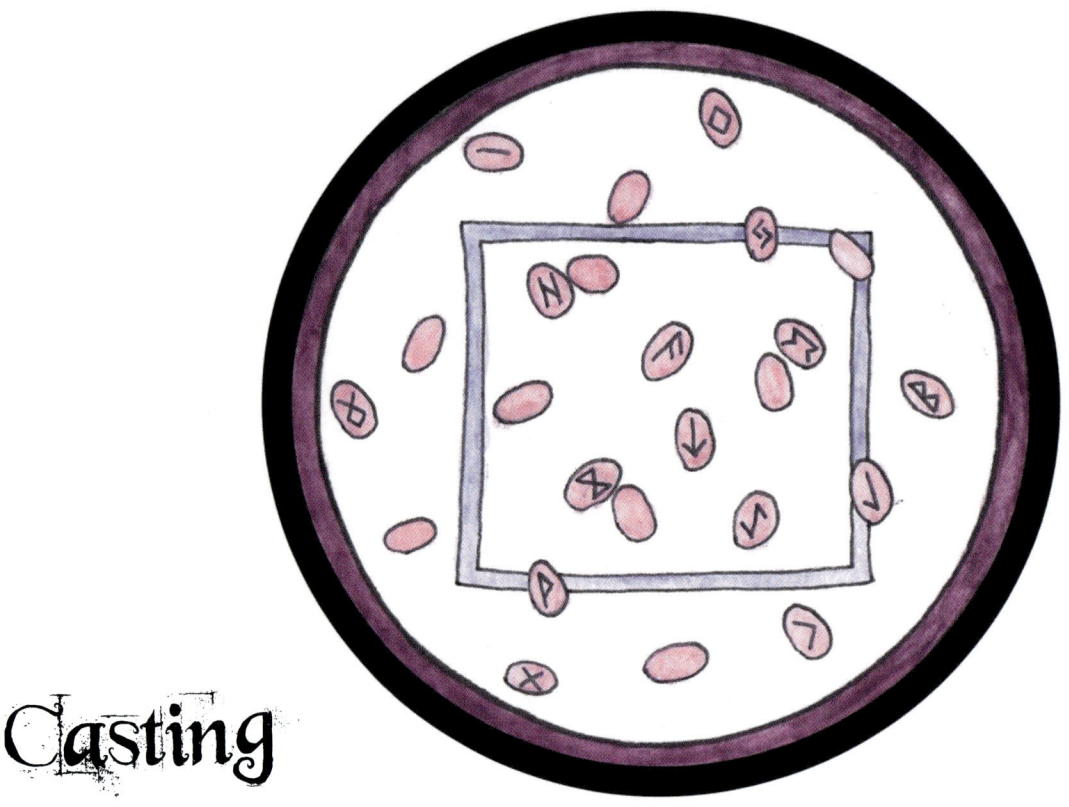

Casting

Now that you've created your own set of runes, let's learn how to use them.

Reading runes is called Casting. Casting runes is a type of magic called Divination. It is similar to reading Tarot cards. It is a way to help you predict the future and solve problems. There are two ways to do rune castings, Throwing and Rune Spreads. Casting runes can be complicated, so we're going to learn the simplest methods. You should also be familiar with the meanings of each rune.

Before you do a rune casting you should always make sure that you are feeling your best. Just before you begin, you will want to take a moment to close your eyes, clear your mind and steady your breathing. You may also ask Odin for guidance during your casting.

Throwing

Get a square white cloth to cast your runes on. It should be about 18 inches by 18 inches in size. Draw two circles on your white cloth, like in the picture below:

When you're ready to begin your casting, ask your question or state your concerns out loud. Think of one rune that relates to your question. If this rune shows up in your reading, circumstances may not change.

Pour your runes out onto your cloth about one foot above the center circle. Any runes that are face down can be put back into the bag. Any runes that land off of the cloth can also be put back in the bag. (More advanced Runemasters may choose to read all of the runes, including the ones that land outside of the cloth. It takes a great deal of practice to use this technique.)

Here are two ways you can read this casting:

Outcome, Solution, Problem

Inner Circle: These runes can help you find out exactly what your issue is based on your question or concerns.

Middle Circle: These runes will help you solve your issue.

Outer Circle: These runes can tell you the likely outcome if you follow the runes' advice.

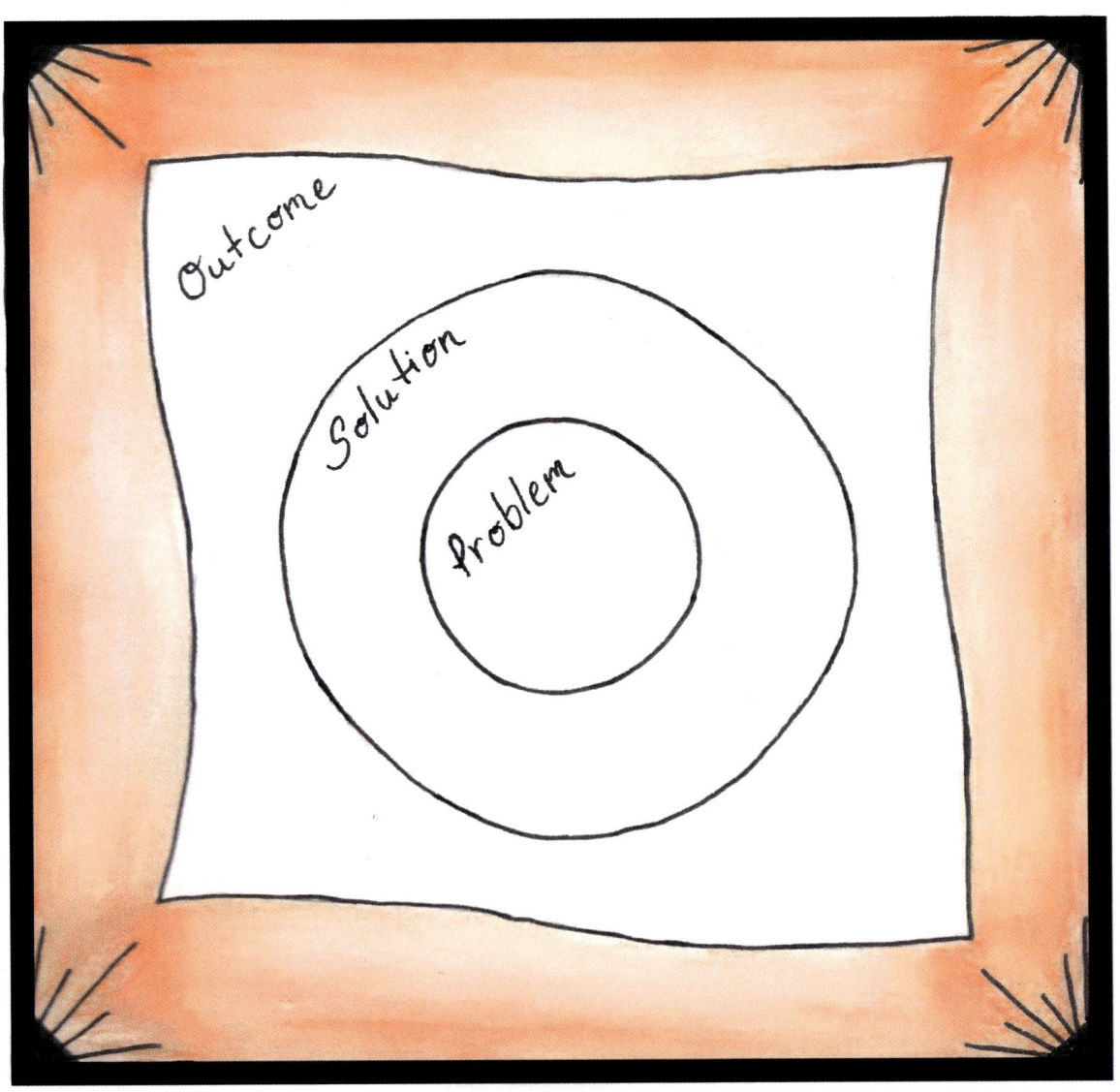

Past, Present, Future

(You don't need to have a question for this to gain general knowledge, but it's okay if you do have a specific question.)

Inner Circle: These runes show the issues you have had in the past or your past experiences.

Middle Circle: These runes show what is going on in your life right now.

Outer Circle: These runes can show you what can happen in your future.

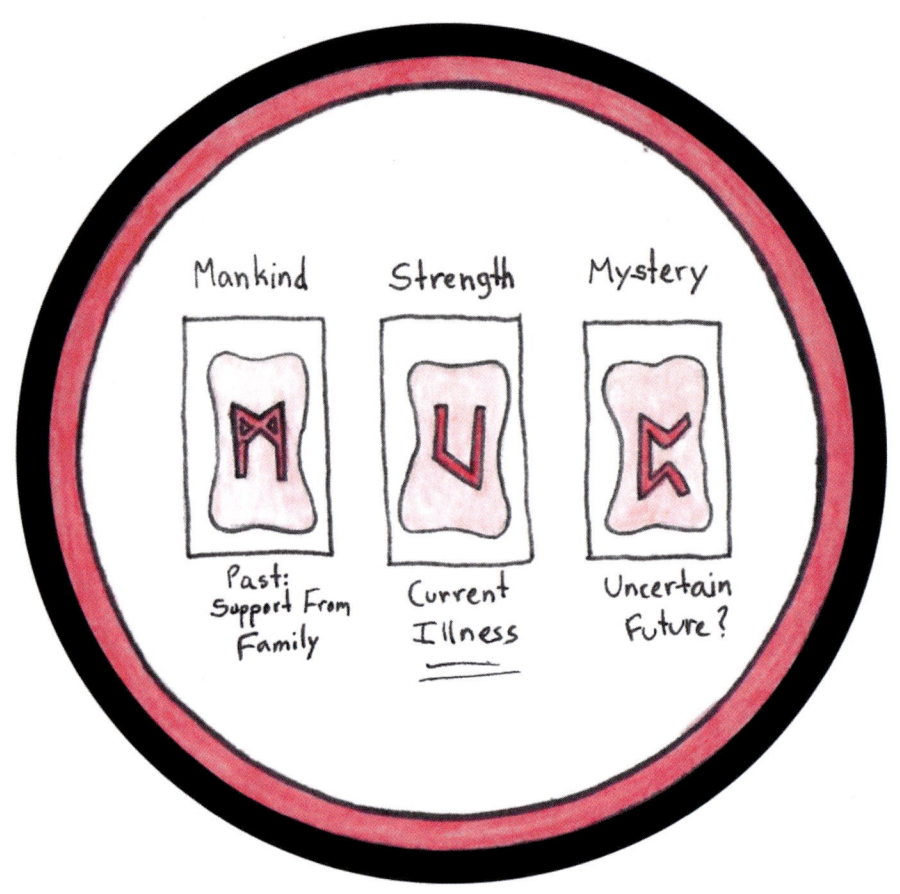

Rune Spreads

A rune spread is a fixed position that you place runes on after pulling them out of the bag. There are many rune spreads that you can use; some are simple, and some are very complex. We will learn five simple spreads.

Single Rune Spread

These are best for when you have a "yes or no" question. For example:

"Should I ask the new student in my class to be my friend?"

"Will I do something exciting today?"

Clear your mind, think of your question, and reach into your rune bag. Let your intuition guide you to a rune. Do not purposely feel the shape of a rune if you are using carved runes. That's cheating. Carefully pull out one rune, making sure that you do not flip it over. If the rune comes out facedown the answer is No, which means face up is Yes. If it is face up, you may choose to take into consideration the meaning and position of the rune.

Another way to do a single rune spread is to pull a rune out of the bag each morning, carry it with you (if you want to), and let it guide you throughout your day.

Three Rune Spreads

Use these spreads if you are looking for deeper guidance.

These are, "How can I-" or "What should I do-", type questions.

"How can I get a promotion at work?"

"What should I do about my best friend's new friend?"

In this spread, you will pull three runes out of the bag, one at a time. They will be placed in certain spots that have a special meaning. It is similar to the circles on the cloth for throwing. To make it easier to read, you can take a piece of printer paper, turn it sideways, and draw three rectangles like this:

There are several types of three rune spreads. We are going to start off with two.

Problem, Action, Outcome

Place One: This is a problem or issue you are having. The rune will tell you what it is.

Place Two: This is what you need to do to solve your problem.

Place Three: This tells you what can happen if you follow the advice from the rune on place two.

Past, Present, Future

No question or issue is necessarily needed for this spread. It is a general reading for your current time in life. It can help guide you into the future.

Now that you have learned about one rune spreads and three rune spreads, we will take it one step further and learn four rune spreads.

Four Rune Spreads

Four Seasons Spread

Your first rune goes in the box of which season you are in. If you are in the season of Spring, your first rune goes there. If you are in the season of Winter, your first rune will go in the "Winter" box, Spring is #2, Summer is #3, and Autumn is #4. The rotation is clockwise. This spread can help you know what to expect for the rest of the year, no matter what season you are in.

Wishing Spread

Get your question ready!

Place One: tells you about your past wishes that have something to do with your question.

Place Two: tells you about your current wishes and how you are feeling about your problem or issue.

Place Three: tells you about how others, your friends and family, feel about your problem or issue and what their wishes are for you.

Place Four: tells you what your deepest desire is, what you wish for the most, even if you are keeping it a secret.

This spread can help you figure out what you want the most in your life at the time that you cast this spread.

See Illustration on the next page >

Master these rune spreads and you will be able to learn even more as your journey continues!

Rune Magic

Besides Divination, runes can also be used in spells! Before using the runes for magic, you really need to know all about each rune, so study hard! Here, we will cover some simple rune magic.

The Eight Steps in Rune Magic

1. Pick what type of material you will be using. It is traditional to use wood.
2. Carefully carve your runes. Make sure you fully understand the meaning of each rune, otherwise you may use the wrong one and have an undesired outcome.
3. If you are carving into wood, use red paint inside your carving. If you wish not to carve, you can simply paint your runes of choice.
4. Ask for a blessing from the God or Goddess who rules over the meaning of the rune. Or you can ask Odin, as he is the first Runemaster.
5. Speak out loud what your intentions are for your runes. Tell them what you want them to do.
6. Take your finger, or a wand, and trace a circle around your talisman or amulet three times. Picture that circle in your mind. This will seal the magic inside.
7. Hold the rune tight, putting your energy into it. Send the power to whomever, or whatever, you are making it for, even if it is for yourself.
8. Now that you are finished, close your magical session. You can say something simple like, "My work here is done, so let it be."

When your spell has worked, or even if it hasn't, give your talisman a resting place. You can bury it or release it into a lake or the beach.

Talismans & Amulets

Talismans are used to draw power to you. Amulets are used for protection. A Talisman or an Amulet is something that you can wear or carry. It can be a piece of jewelry, a stone or a wood carving, that can bring you protection or good luck. By drawing or carving a rune onto your talisman or amulet you are telling that rune that you need help with something.

Protection Amulet

If you feel that you need to be protected from something or someone you can turn to the rune Algiz. Algiz is the most powerful for protection.

Your Algiz protection amulet can look something like this:

A stone that you asked permission to take from nature

A twig that was found on the ground, no longer needed by its tree

Maybe you have a favorite necklace that you can draw on the back of the pendant?

Algiz is a great start for protecting yourself, but you may want protection from something specific. For example:

- Algiz for Protection
- Hagalaz means hail. Hail comes from a storm.

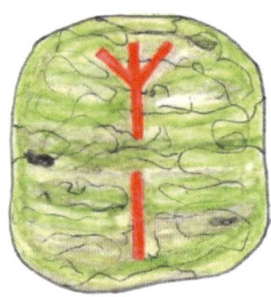

- Algiz for Protection
- Isa means Ice and also Danger

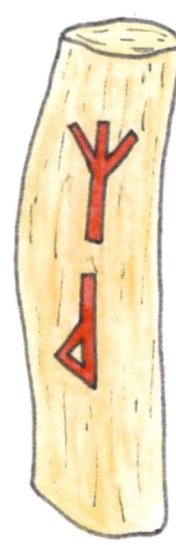

Protection from a Broken Heart
- Algiz for Protection
- Reversed Wunjo for Heartbreak

Good Luck Charm (Talisman)

Need a little boost to brighten your day? These are a few runes that you can carry or wear.

Bring Dagaz with you to feel the warm sunlight and blessings from Baldur!

Carry Berkana when you are feeling nervous about starting something new!

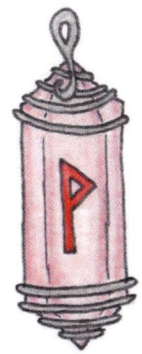

Hold Wunjo close when you need some added happiness and joy!

Keep Fehu with you to encourage wealth and prosperity to come your way!

Bindrune Talisman or Amulet

A Bindrune is when you join two or more runes together to create a unique meaning. For example:

Ansuz - ᚨ

Ehwaz - ᛖ

This combination can be worn to aid in communication

Carry this as a Talisman with you when you have a school presentation or when you need to have a long talk with family or friends.

Runic Formulas

A Runic Formula is the name of a God or Goddess, or Old Norse words that are carved or painted onto a talisman.

There are many Gods and Goddesses, all who have extraordinary qualities and powers. You may write the name of a God or Goddess in runes onto your talisman to gain those qualities and powers.

Snotra is a Goddess of wisdom, intelligence and prudence. You can call upon these qualities, say, if you have a big exam coming up.

ᛋᚾᛟᛏᚱᚨ is Snotra written in runes. This is what you would carve or paint onto your talisman.

Thor is a God of loyalty. If you are looking to gain loyal friends, his name can be carved or painted onto your talisman.

ᚦᛟᚱ is Thor written in runes.

Strength in Old Norse is kraptr and can be written as ᚲᚱᚨᛈᛏᚱ

Murkstave Runes

(Also called Reversed Runes)

What if my rune is upside down?

There are positive and negative meanings of runes. Some runes cannot be reversed, but if the other runes in the casting are primarily negative/reversed, you may choose to read the reversed meaning for that rune.

In my previous book, "Children's Book of Runes", I only covered the positive meanings, as it is meant for all ages, including our youngest readers and learners.

Before attempting to cast or perform rune magic you should deeply familiarize yourself with both meanings. On the Rune Reference pages, you will find basic meanings for regular and murkstave (reversed) positions.

Fehu

Wealth, Good Health, Fortune

Murkstave: Poverty, Greed, Illness

Uruz

Strength, Creative Power, Energy

Murkstave: Hatred, Failure, Lack of Motivation

Thurisaz

Luck, Protection, Transformation

Murkstave: Obstinacy, Pain, Vulnerability

Ansuz

Divine Powers, Wisdom Encouragement

Murkstave: Betrayal, Trickery, Misinformation

Raido

Journey, Changes, Movement/Rhythm

Murkstave: Complications, Delays, Going Astray

Kenaz

Enlightenment, Knowledge, Inner Light

Murkstave: False Hope, Endings, Blockage

Gebo

Generosity, Good Luck, Friendship

(Not Reversible) Negative Meaning: Dishonesty, Codependency, Unbalance

Wunjo

Joy, Peace, Fulfillment

Murkstave: Unhappiness, Loneliness, Tension

Hagalaz

Limitations, Disruption, Delays

(Not Reversible) Negative Meaning: Chaos, Severity, Great Loss

Nauthiz

Restriction, Responsibility, Need

(Not Reversible) Negative Meaning: Hastiness, Ill Desires, Destructive Behaviors

Isa

Stagnation, Obstacles, Renewal

(Not Reversible) Negative Meaning: Impatience, Danger, Deception

Jera

Growth, Cycles, Harvest

(Not Reversible) Negative Meaning: Bad Karma, Negative Cycles, Barrenness

Eihwaz

Rebirth, Defense, Transition

(Not Reversible)
Negative Meaning: Death, Old Problems Return, Confusion

Pertho

Secrets/Mystery, Games/Fun, Revelation

Murkstave: Melancholy, Disappointments, Risk-taking

Algiz

Best Protection, Opportunity, Assistance

Murkstave: Defenselessness, Poor Health, Caution

Sowelo

Confidence, Success, Love, Guidance

(Not Reversible)
Negative Meaning: One's Dark Side, Burnout, Overconfidence

Tiwaz

Victory, Justice, Honor, Courage

Murkstave: Cowardice, Defeat, Injustice

Berkana

Birth, New Happiness, Family

Murkstave: Dormancy, Infertility, Carelessness

Ehwaz
Loyalty, Travel, Partnerships

Murkstave: Recklessness, Broken Boundaries, Stagnation

Mannaz

Community, Human Potential, Intelligence

Murkstave: No Inspiration, Self-reliance, Isolation

Laguz

Intuition, Psychic Ability, Emotions

Murkstave: Misjudgement, Spiritual Blockages, Depression

Inguz

Gratification, Fertile Mind, Completion

(Not Reversible)
Negative Meaning: Missed Opportunities, Guilty Pleasure, Instability

Othila

Inheritance, Ancestral Land, Homecoming

Murkstave: Displacement, Family Disputes, Loss

Dagaz

Insight, Balance, Breakthroughs

(Not Reversible)
Negative Meaning: Problem Dwelling, Need Balance, Rough Transition

Alphabet Reference

Fehu – F,V ᚠ

Uruz – U ᚢ

Thurisaz – TH ᚦ

Ansuz – A ᚨ

Raido – R ᚱ

Kenaz – K, C(hard), Q ᚲ

Gebo – G(hard) ᚷ

Wunjo – W ᚹ

Hagalaz – H ᚺ

Nauthiz – N ᚾ

Isa – I ᛁ

Jera – Y,J ᛃ

Eihwaz – E (ee) ᛇ

Pertho – P ᛈ

Algiz – X,Z ᛉ

Sowelo – S, C (soft) ᛋ

Tiwaz – T ᛏ

Berkana – B ᛒ

Ehwaz – E (eh) ᛖ

Mannaz – M ᛗ

Laguz – L ᛚ

Inguz – NG (ing) ᛜ

Othila – O ᛟ

Dagaz – D ᛞ

Thank you for taking the time to read this book! I wish you well on your magical journey!

Made in the USA
Middletown, DE
08 December 2023

45038881R00018